The Bridge Is Love

The Bridge Is Love

Words of Comfort, Messages of Hope

Selected by Dean Walley

The C. R. Gibson Company
Norwalk, Connecticut

"Soon we shall die . . . and we ourselves
shall be loved for a while and forgotten.
But the love will have been enough;
all those impulses of love return
to the love that made them. Even
memory is not necessary for love.
There is a land of the living and
a land of the dead and the bridge is love,
the only survival, the only meaning."

THORNTON WILDER

HE WHO ASKED

He who asked: 'Who knows
The meaning of the snow?'
Is answered now.
'Who understands the rose?'
Is shown its mystery.

'What is that long night,
The dark day of the dead?'
To him who said
'Let me see Love,' the secret sight
Is simply told, once whispered in agony.

JAMES KIRKUP

They that love beyond the world cannot be separated.
Death cannot kill what never dies. Nor can Spirits ever be
divided that love and live in the same Divine Principle; the
Root and Record of their Friendship. Death is but crossing
the world, as Friends do the Seas; they live in one another still.

WILLIAM PENN

WITH LOVE

He who fears death fears life and walks in fear,
Wailing and reckoning down his portioned days
Like one condemned to die. Beloved dear,
It is not so with me who know death's ways
(Who quickly learned), I say it is not so;
Love which was strong in life, in death as strong,
Would have me sing the slow, long road I go—
For short or long, I say the road is long.
And yet I journey light, for it is sweet
To mourn you singing, make of every mile
(Of every anguish), one the less—O feet
That falter not, lips that still dare the smile,
Hands, crowning every common thing they do
With love of you, with very love of you.

LEONORA SPEYER

Love stands opposed to death. It is love, not reason, that is stronger than death. Only love, not reason, gives sweet thoughts. And from love and sweetness alone can form come; form and civilization, friendly, enlightened, beautiful human intercourse,—always in silent recognition of the blood-sacrifice. . . . I will keep faith with death in my heart, yet well remember that faith with death and the dead is evil, is hostile to humankind, so soon as we give it power over thought and action. *For the sake of goodness and love, man shall let death have no sovereignty over his thoughts.*

THOMAS MANN

Death is far more than a natural process. It is but the outward sign of a much greater reality. The last great sacrament of which we can only partake once; for which all life should be a preparation; and therefore when it comes we do not need to be brave, as in the presence of a foe, but we stretch out our hands in welcome as to a friend we have "long abideth and looked after." And in death we meet the Conqueror of death; we meet Love.

F. M. M. COMPER

In this selection from "War and Peace", Prince Andrey, mortally wounded at the battle of Borodino, knows that there is no eternity apart from love.

'Yes, love (he thought again with perfect distinctness), but not that love that loves for something, to gain something, or because of something, but that love that I felt for the first time, when dying, I saw my enemy and yet loved him. I knew that feeling of love which is the very essence of the soul, for which no object is needed. And I know that blissful feeling now too. To love one's neighbours; to love one's enemies. To love everything—to love God in all His manifestations. Some one dear to one can be loved with human love; but an enemy can only be loved with divine love. And that was why I felt such joy when I felt that I loved that man. What happened to him? Is he alive? . . . Loving with human love, one may pass from love to hatred; but divine love cannot change. Nothing, not even death, nothing can shatter it. It is the very nature of the soul. . . .

'Love is life. All, all that I understand, I understand only because I love. All is, all exists only because I love. All is bound up in love alone. Love is God, and dying means for me a particle of love, to go back to the universal and eternal source of love.'

LEO TOLSTOY

For the first sharp pangs there is no comfort; whatever goodness may surround us, darkness and silence still hang about our pain. But slowly, the clinging companionship with the dead is linked with our living affections and duties, and we begin to feel our sorrow as a solemn initiation, preparing us for that sense of loving, pitying fellowship with the fullest human lot, which I must think, no one who has tasted it will deny to be the chief blessedness of our life.

GEORGE ELIOT

BEYOND

It seemeth such a little way to me
    Across to that strange country, —the Beyond;
And yet not strange, for it has grown to be
    The home of those of whom I am most fond;
They make it seem familiar and most dear,
    As journeying friends bring distant regions near. . . .

And so for me there is no sting to death,
    And so the grave has lost its victory,
It is but crossing, —with abated breath,
    And white, set face, —a little strip of sea,
To find the loved ones waiting on the shore,
    More beautiful, more precious than before.

ELLA WHEELER WILCOX

THE SOUL'S INVINCIBLE SURMISE

O world, thou choosest not the better part!
It is not wisdom to be only wise,
And on the inward vision close the eyes;
But it is wisdom to believe the heart.
Columbus found a world, and had no chart
Save one that faith deciphered in the skies;
To trust the soul's invincible surmise
Was all his science and his only art.
Our knowledge is a torch of smoky pine
That lights the pathway but one step ahead
Across a void of mystery and dread.
Bid, then, the tender light of faith to shine
By which alone to mortal heart is led
Unto the thinking of the thought divine.

GEORGE SANTAYANA

And as a goldsmith, taking a piece of gold, turns it into another, newer and more beautiful shape, so does this Self, after having thrown off this body and dispelled all ignorance, make unto himself another, newer and more beautiful shape.

UPANISHAD

Because we cannot see our loved ones after death, does not mean they cease to be.

Cecil B. deMille, famed motion picture producer and director, was a sensitive, spiritually-minded man. He said that one summer day he was in Maine, in a canoe on a lake deep in the woods. He was alone. He wanted to think, so let the canoe drift idly. Suddenly he discovered that he was in shallow water about four inches deep near the shore, and he could plainly see a number of water beetles on the lake bottom. One of them crawled out of the water onto the canoe and sank its talons into the woodwork of the hull, and there it died. Three hours later, still drifting in the sun, deMille observed a wondrous miracle. He noticed that the shell of the water beetle was cracking open. A moist head emerged, followed by wings. Finally the winged creature left the dead body and flew into the air, going farther in one-half second than the water beetle could crawl all day. It was a dragonfly, its beautiful colors shimmering in the sunlight. The dragonfly flew above the surface of the water, but the water beetles below could not see it. They were unaware of their glorious future in new birth.

Can we reason logically that Almighty God would effect that wonderful change for a water beetle and would not work such transformation for us?

NORMAN VINCENT PEALE

The immortality of the soul is a thing which concerns us so mightily, which touches us so deeply, that it is necessary to have lost all feeling in order to be indifferent about it. All our actions and thoughts must take different paths according as there will be or will not be eternal goods to be hoped for, so that it is impossible to do anything with intelligence and judgment, if it is not regulated by the view of that point which ought to be our final object.

BLAISE PASCAL

If there were no future life,
our souls would not thirst for it.

JEAN PAUL RICHTER

Our Creator would never have made such lovely days, and have given us the deep hearts to enjoy them, above and beyond all thought, unless we were meant to be immortal.

NATHANIEL HAWTHORNE

IMMORTALITY

I do not have the power to prove that man is immortal and that the soul exists; but I know that there must be such a proof, and that compared with it every other demonstration is idle. It is true that human life without immortality would be inconceivable to me, though that is not the ground for my belief.

My belief in immortality, so far as I can divine its origin, and that is not far, seems to be connected with the same impulse which urges me to know myself. I can never know myself, but the closer I come to knowledge of myself the more certain I must feel that I am immortal, and, conversely, the more certain I am of my immortality the more intimately I must come to know myself. For I shall attend and listen to a class of experiences which the disbeliever in immortality ignores or dismisses as irrelevant to temporal life. The experiences I mean are of little practical use and have no particular economic or political interest. They come when I am least aware of myself as a personality moulded by my will and time: in moments of contemplation when I am unconscious of my body, or indeed that I have a body with separate members; in moments of grief or prostration; in happy hours with friends; and, because self-forgetfulness is most complete then, in dreams and day-dreams and in that floating, half-discarnate state which precedes and follows sleep. In these hours there seems to me to be knowledge of my real self and simultaneously knowledge of immortality.

EDWIN MUIR

Two children were overheard talking about the death of their grandmother. The five-year-old girl was asking her seven-year-old brother how "grandmother went to God." "Well," said the boy, "it happened this way. First Grandmother reached up and up and up as far as she could. Then God reached down and down and down. When their hands touched, he took her."

GENE E. BARTLETT

Much of our horror of death comes from the feeling (even though it may never be expressed) that it is the enemy of life. We love life; therefore it is natural to dread death. But death is no more the enemy of life than sleep is the enemy of work and play. Sleep makes it possible for us to work and play the next day. Death makes it possible for us to live on. It has therefore a real contribution to make to life in the large, being the gateway through which we slip from the lower life into the higher, from the briefer into that which is eternal.

UNKNOWN

Many people seem to feel that science has somehow made "religious ideas" untimely or old-fashioned. But I think science has a real surprise for the skeptics. Science, for instance, tells us that nothing in nature, not even the tiniest particle, can disappear without a trace. Nature does not know extinction. All it knows is transformation.

Now, if God applies this fundamental principle to the most minute and insignificant parts of His universe, doesn't it make sense to assume that He applies it also to the human soul? I think it does. And everything science has taught me—and continues to teach me—strengthens my belief in the continuity of our spiritual existence after death. Nothing disappears without a trace.

WERNHER VON BRAUN

I know only scientifically determined truth,
but I am going to believe
what I wish to believe,
what I cannot help but believe—
I expect to meet this dear child in another world.

LOUIS PASTEUR

Our lives are waves that come up out of the ocean of eternity, break upon the beach of earth, and lapse back to the ocean of eternity. Some are sunlit, some run in storm and rain; one is a quiet ripple, another is a thunderous breaker; and once in many centuries comes a great tidal wave that sweeps over a continent; but all go back to the sea and lie equally level there.

AUSTIN O'MALLEY

Death is not extinguishing
the light; it is putting out
the lamp because the dawn
has come.

SIR RABINDRANATH TAGORE

THESE TOO, I LEAVE TO YOU!

But how can I live without you?—she cried.
    I left all world to you when I died:
    Beauty of earth and air and sea;
    Leap of a swallow or a tree;
    Kiss of rain and wind's embrace;
    Passion of storm and winter's face;
    Touch of feather, flower and stone;
    Chiselled line of branch or bone;
    Flight of stars, night's caravan;
    Song of crickets—and of man—
All these I put in my testament,
    All these I bequeathed you when I went.

But how can I see them without your eyes
Or touch them without your hand?
How can I hear them without your ear,
Without your heart, understand?

    These too, these too
    I leave to you!

ANNE MORROW LINDBERGH

TO THOSE LEFT BEHIND

I have come through the darkness over the swollen waters,
I have moored my raft at last on a sunlit shore,
But I hear your weeping . . . Oh my sisters, my brothers,
Weep no more!

For how can I go on while your hearts are breaking?
There is a golden light on the land ahead;
The winds are cool and sweet, I am strong for climbing,
I am not dead!

I shall leave my raft on the old sea's sandy reaches,
I shall make my way along a glittering track;
I shall be wild with joy . . . unless your crying
Should call me back.

Even here it hurts, oh my brothers, my sisters,
To know that you still are bound while I am free,
But let me explore, unhindered, the sparkling meadows
Of Eternity.

GRACE NOLL CROWELL

THERE IS A NEW MORNING

There is a new morning, and a new way,
When the heart wakes in the green
Meadow of its choice, and the feet stray
Securely on their new-found paths, unseen,
Unhindered in the certain light of day.

There is a new time, and a new word
That is the timeless dream of uncreated speech.
When the heart beats for the first time, like a bird
Battering the bright boughs of its tree; when each
To the other turns, all prayers are heard.

There is a new world, and a new man
Who walks amazed that he so long
Was blind, and dumb; he who now towards the sun
Lifts up a trustful face in skilful song,
And fears no more the darkness where his day began.

JAMES KIRKUP

When Dr. Edward A. Wilson was lost with Captain Robert Falcon Scott on their ill-fated expedition to Antarctica, he left a brave heritage for those who face the storms of life and death today. Dr. Wilson sensed above the breathtaking blasts of cold wind and the thudding of his benumbed feet that he would not arrive home safely. Before he perished on the paralyzing ice, he pencilled this note to his loved ones: "Don't be unhappy. We are playing a good part in a great scheme arranged by God himself. . . . We will all meet after death, and death has no terrors. . . . All is for the best to those that love God. . . . All is well."

Let us no longer regard a man
as having ceased to live,
although nature suggests it;
but as beginning to live,
as truth assures.

BLAISE PASCAL

You must not grieve for me, for if you really believe in religion and all that it entails that would be hypocrisy. I have no fear of death; only a queer elation. . . . I would have it no other way. The universe is so vast and so ageless that the life of one man can only be justified by the measure of his sacrifice. We are sent to this world to acquire a personality and a character to take with us that can never be taken from us. Those who just eat and sleep, prosper and procreate, are no better than animals if all their lives they are at peace.

I firmly and absolutely believe that evil things are sent into the world to try us; they are sent deliberately by our Creator to test our mettle because He knows what is good for us. The Bible is full of cases where the easy way out has been discarded for moral principles.

I count myself fortunate in that I have seen the whole country and known men of every calling. But with the final test of war I consider my character fully developed. Thus at my early age my mission is already fulfilled and I am prepared to die with just one regret, and one only, —that I could not devote myself to making your declining years more happy by being with you; but you will live in peace and freedom, and I shall have directly contributed to that, so here again my life will not have been in vain.

FROM A BRITISH AVIATOR'S LAST
LETTER TO HIS MOTHER

THE VISION OF PARADISE

Dark was that impenetrable door
At which we stood like shades
Waiting for admission. Then we saw
Our real shadows melt into the rock
Like sun, or wind, or rain piercing the spring's white glades.
And naturally, with no loss, no sense of shock
Or shame, we found ourselves, at last,
Re-entering the dwelling that our faith had lost.

There all was bright with sunlight and profusions.
Our shrunken hearts delighted to be rich again
With all the tender savagery of continents and oceans.
We could feel the wild blood burning in each living hand,
The breath of gods and heroes flowing in each vein.
We had entered life as if a new-found land
Had suddenly appeared familiar, and good.
And there was speech, like love, which all men understood.

JAMES KIRKUP

MYSTERIES

But this we know: our loved and dead, if they should come
    this day—
Should come and ask us, "What is life?"—not one of us
    could say,
Life is a mystery, as deep as ever death can be;
Yet, oh, how dear it is to us, this life we live and see!

Then might they say—these vanished ones—and blessed is the
    thought,
"So death is sweet to us, beloved! though we may show you
    naught;
We may not to the quick reveal the mystery of death—
Ye cannot tell us, if ye would, the mystery of breath!"

The child who enters life comes not with knowledge or intent,
So those who enter death must go as little children sent.
Nothing is known. But I believe that God is overhead;
And as life is to the living, so death is to the dead.

MARY MAPES DODGE

THE HEAVENLY CITY

I sigh for the heavenly country,
Where the heavenly people pass,
And the sea is as quiet as a mirror
Of beautiful beautiful glass.

I walk in the heavenly field,
With lilies and poppies bright,
I am dressed in a heavenly coat
Of polished white.

When I walk in the heavenly parkland
My feet on the pasture are bare,
Tall waves the grass, but no harmful
Creature is there.

At night I fly over the housetops,
And stand on the bright moony beams;
Gold are all heaven's rivers
And silver her streams.

STEVIE SMITH

Blessed are they that mourn:
for they shall be comforted.

MATTHEW 5:4

Bereavement is the deepest initiation into the mysteries of human life, an initiation more searching and profound than even happy love. Love remembered and consecrated by grief belongs, more clearly than the happy intercourse of friends, to the eternal world; it has proved itself stronger than death.

Bereavement is the sharpest challenge to our trust in God; if faith can overcome this, there is no mountain which it cannot remove. And faith can overcome it. It brings the eternal world nearer to us, and makes it seem more real.

DEAN INGE

THE SHIP

I am standing upon the seashore. A ship at my side spreads her white sails to the morning breeze and starts for the blue ocean.

She is an object of beauty and strength, and I stand and watch her until at length she is only a speck of white cloud just where the sea and sky meet and mingle with each other. Then someone at my side exclaims, "There, she's gone!"

Gone where? Gone from my sight, that is all. She is just as large in hull and mast and spar as she was when she left my side, and just as able to bear her load of living freight to the place of her destination. Her diminished size is in me, not in her.

And just at the moment when someone at my side says, "She's gone," there are other eyes watching for her coming and other voices ready to take up the glad shout, "There, she comes!"

And that is dying.

UNKNOWN

I will lift up mine eyes unto the hills,
from whence cometh my help.
My help cometh from the Lord,
which made heaven and earth.
He will not suffer thy foot to be moved:
he that keepeth thee will not slumber.
Behold, he that keepeth Israel
shall neither slumber nor sleep.
The Lord is thy keeper:
the Lord is thy shade upon thy right hand.
The sun shall not smite thee by day,
nor the moon by night.
The Lord shall preserve thee from all evil:
he shall preserve thy soul.
The Lord shall preserve thy going out
and thy coming in from this time forth,
and even for evermore.

PSALM 121

Sonia.

I may be just as unhappy as you, but I don't give way to despair. I can bear it and I shall go on bearing it until my life comes to its natural end. You must bear it, too.

Uncle Vanya.

My child, I'm so unhappy! Oh, if only you knew how unhappy I am!

Sonia.

It can't be helped, we must go on living however unhappy we are! We shall go on living, Uncle Vanya. We shall live through a long, long round of days and dreary evenings; we shall bear with patience the trials which fate has in store for us; we shall work without resting for others now and in our old age, and when our time comes, we shall die without complaining; and there, beyond the grave, we shall say that we have wept and suffered, that we had a hard, bitter struggle; and God will have pity on us, and you and I, Uncle dear, will see a new life, a bright, lovely, and happy life; and we shall rejoice and shall look back with a deep feeling of tenderness and a smile upon our present sufferings and tribulations, and—and we shall rest. . . . I believe that, Uncle, fervently, passionately believe it! We shall rest! We shall hear the angels; we shall see all heaven bright with many stars, shining like diamonds; we shall see all our sufferings and all earthly evil dissolve in mercy that will fill the whole world, and our life will be peaceful, tender, and sweet as a caress. I believe that, I do, I believe it. Poor, poor Uncle Vanya, you are crying. . . . You knew no happiness in your life, but wait, Uncle Vanya, wait. . . . We shall rest. . . . We shall rest!

ANTON CHEKHOV

from '*Uncle Vanya*'

ACCEPTANCE

When the spent sun throws up its rays on cloud
And goes down burning into the gulf below,
No voice in nature is heard to cry aloud
At what has happened. Birds, at least, must know
It is the change to darkness in the sky.
Murmuring something quiet in her breast,
One bird begins to close a faded eye;
Or overtaken too far from his nest,
Hurrying low above the grove, some waif
Swoops just in time to his remembered tree.
At most he thinks or twitters softly, "Safe!
Now let the night be dark for all of me.
Let the night be too dark for me to see
Into the future. Let what will be, be."

ROBERT FROST

In the following passage, Dr. Viktor Frankl, founder of the school of Logotherapy, tells how suffering is eased when we find meaning in our loss.

Whenever one is confronted with an inescapable, unavoidable situation, whenever one has to face a fate which cannot be changed, e.g., an incurable disease, such as an inoperable cancer; just then one is given a last chance to actualize the highest value, to fulfill the deepest meaning, the meaning of suffering. For what matters above all is the attitude we take toward suffering, the attitude in which we take our suffering upon ourselves.

Let me cite a clear-cut example: Once, an elderly general practitioner consulted me because of his severe depression. He could not overcome the loss of his wife who had died two years before and whom he had loved above all else. Now how could I help him? What should I tell him? Well, I refrained from telling him anything but instead confronted him with the question, "What would have happened, Doctor, if you had died first, and your wife would have had to survive you?" "Oh," he said, "for her this would have been terrible; how she would have suffered!" Whereupon I replied, "You see, Doctor, such a suffering has been spared her, and it was you who have spared her this suffering; but now, you have to pay for it by surviving and mourning her." He said no word but shook my hand and calmly left my office. Suffering ceases to be suffering in some way at the moment it finds a meaning, such as the meaning of a sacrifice.

I beg you, if God sends you grief, to take it largely by
letting it first of all show you how short life is, and then
prophesy eternity. Such is the grief of which the poet sings so
nobly:

Grief should be
Like joy, majestic, equable, sedate;
Confirming, cleansing, raising, making free;
Strong to consume small troubles, to command
Great thoughts, grave thoughts,
thoughts lasting to the end.

But grief, to be all that, must see the end; must bring and
forever keep with its pain such a sense of the shortness of
life that the pain shall seem but a temporary accident, and
all that is to stay for ever after the pain has ceased, the
exaltation, the unselfishness, the mystery, the nearness of
God, shall seem to be the substance of the sorrow.

PHILLIPS BROOKS

I have come to understand that we see only a small part of the whole pattern of existence. Sorrow and suffering give opportunities for growth. Disappointment often opens doors to wider fields. The tragedy of death, as someone wiser than I has said, is separation, but even separation may not be permanent. The sense of continuing companionship with those who have gone beyond the horizon which comes to me occasionally makes me confident that someday we shall see beyond the mystery which now we must accept. Often it seems that those who have most to give to the world are the very ones who are taken from it in the flower of their youth and vigor. It is hard to understand why this should be so, unless—and this I believe to be true—they have done whatever it was they had to do here, have fulfilled their secret contract with this world, and have been released for more important work elsewhere.

ELIZABETH GRAY VINING

For every thing there is a season,
and a time for every matter under heaven:
A time to be born, and a time to die;
a time to plant, and a time to pluck up that which is planted;
A time to kill, and a time to heal;
a time to break down, and a time to build up;
A time to weep, and a time to laugh;
a time to mourn, and a time to dance;
A time to cast away stones, and a time to gather stones
    together;
a time to embrace, and a time to refrain from embracing;
A time to get, and a time to lose;
a time to keep, and a time to cast away;
A time to rend, and a time to sew;
a time to keep silence, and a time to speak.

ECCLESIASTES 3:1-7

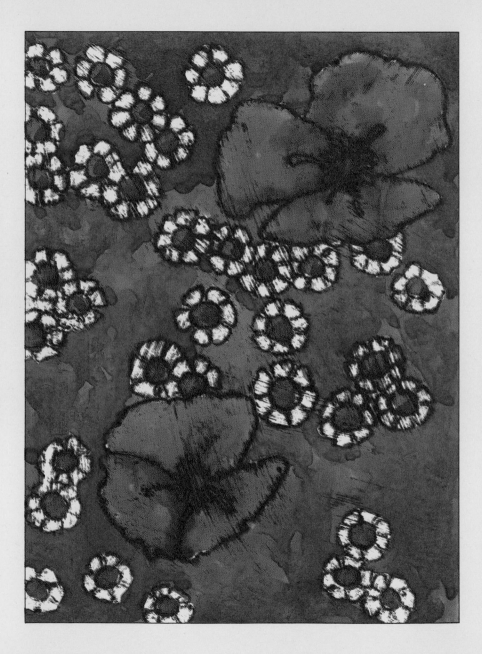

"Something has spoken to me in the night, burning the tapers of the waning year; something has spoken in the night, and told me I shall die, I know not where. Saying:

" 'To lose the earth you know, for greater knowing; to lose the life you have, for greater life; to leave the friends you loved, for greater loving; to find a land more kind than home, more large than earth—

" '—Whereon the pillars of this earth are founded, toward which the conscience of the world is tending—a wind is rising, and the rivers flow.' "

THOMAS WOLFE

Dr. Felix Martí-Ibanez in "A Doctor Looks at Death" wrote:

It might help to dissipate our fear if we remember that, were we endowed with consciousness before birth, we would probably feel the same fear of the unknown when passing . . . into the light. . . .

GLIMPSES

I saw a star flame in the sky,
I heard a wild bird sing,
And down where all the forest stirred
Another answering.

All suddenly I felt the gleam
That made my faith revive:
Ah God, it takes such simple things
To keep the soul alive.

HAROLD VINAL

WEEP NOT, WEEP NOT . . .
GO DOWN DEATH

Weep not, weep not,
She is not dead;
She's resting in the bosom of Jesus.
Heartbroken husband—weep no more;
Grief-stricken son—weep no more;
Left-lonesome daughter—weep no more;
She's only just gone home.

Day before yesterday morning,
God was looking down from his great, high heaven,
Looking down on all his children,
And his eye fell on Sister Caroline,
Tossing on her bed of pain,
And God's big heart was touched with pity,
With the everlasting pity.

And God sat back on his throne,
And he commanded that tall, bright angel standing at his
        right hand:
Call me Death!
And that tall bright angel cried in a voice
That broke like a clap of thunder:
Call Death!—Call Death!
And the echo sounded down the streets of heaven
Till it reached away back to that shadowy place,
Where Death waits with his pale, white horses.

And Death heard the summons,
And he leaped on his fastest horse,
Pale as a sheet in the moonlight,
Up the golden street Death galloped,
And the hoofs of his horse struck fire from the gold,
But they didn't make no sound.
Up Death rode to the Great White Throne,
And waited for God's command.

And God said: Go down, Death, go down.
Go down to Savannah, Georgia,
Down in Yamarcraw,
And find Sister Caroline.
She's borne the burden and heat of the day,
She's labored long in my vineyard,
And she's tired—
She's weary—
Go down, Death, and bring her to me.

And Death didn't say a word,
But he loosed the reins on his pale, white horse,
And he clamped the spurs to his bloodless sides,
And out and down he rode,
Through heaven's pearly gates,
Past suns and moons and stars;
On Death rode,
And the foam from his horse was like a comet in the sky;
On Death rode,
Leaving the lightning's flash behind;
Straight on down he came.

While we were watching round her bed,
She turned her eyes and looked away,
She saw what we couldn't see;
She saw Old Death. She saw Old Death,
Coming like a falling star.
But Death didn't frighten Sister Caroline;
He looked to her like a welcome friend.
And she whispered to us: I'm going home,
And she smiled and closed her eyes.

And Death took her up like a baby,
And she lay in his icy arms,
But she didn't feel no chill.
And Death began to ride again—
Up beyond the evening star,
Out beyond the morning star,
Into the glittering light of glory,
On to the Great White Throne.
And there he laid Sister Caroline
On the loving breast of Jesus.

And Jesus took his own hand and wiped away her tears,
And he smoothed the furrows from her face,
And the angels sang a little song,
And Jesus rocked her in his arms,
And kept a-saying: Take your rest,
Take your rest, take your rest.

Weep not—weep not,
She is not dead;
She's resting in the bosom of Jesus.

JAMES WELDON JOHNSON

Life is a voyage that's homeward bound.

HEAVEN OVERARCHES EARTH
AND SEA

Heaven overarches earth and sea,
    Earth-sadness and sea-bitterness.
Heaven overarches you and me:
A little while and we shall be—
Please God—where there is no more sea
    Nor barren wilderness.

Heaven overarches you and me,
    And all earth's gardens and her graves.
Look up with me, until we see
The day break and the shadows flee.
What though to-night wrecks you and me,
    If so, tomorrow saves?

CHRISTINA GEORGINA ROSSETTI

"The growth-curve of the body rises by gradations from infancy until maturity; growth then remains stationary for a while and then, as bodily and mental decay begins to set in, the body-curve declines with increasing rapidity during middle life and old age. This decline is a healthy, normal state of affairs: death is no more pathological than birth. . . . The growth-line of the immortal spirit is very different. . . . As the one begins to decline, the other normally continues to rise and to develop. Increasing wisdom and ripening judgment are measures of this continuing spiritual growth. At last, as old age approaches, we can begin to observe how the 'free spirit' starts to loosen and detach itself from its bondage to the flesh, until at last the body returns to earth, and the spirit to God who gave it."

HOWARD COLLIER

Vast possibilities suggest themselves to us of an order of existence wholly different from all that we have ever known; what may be the nature of that other life it is impossible to know and it is useless to speculate. Such terms as consciousness, individuality, even personality, are but finite screens which give no adequate clue to the infinite for which they stand. Only this I feel warranted in holding fast to— that the root of my selfhood, the best that is in me, my true and only being, cannot perish. In regard to that the notion of death seems to me to be irrelevant. . . . I let go my hold on the empirical, transient self. I see it perish with the same indifference which the materialist asserts, for whom man is but a compound of physical matter and physical force. It is the real self, the eternal self, upon which I tighten my hold. I affirm the real, the irreducible existence of the essential self, though I know not the how or where of its survival. I affirm that there verily is an eternal divine life, a best beyond the best I can think or imagine. What I retain is the conviction that the spiritual self is an eternal self, and cannot perish.

FELIX ADLER

My doctrine is;
Live that thou mayst desire to live again,—
that is thy duty,—
for in any case thou wilt live again.

FRIEDRICH NIETZSCHE

You see I have some reason to wish that, in a future state, I may not only be as well as I was, but a little better. And I hope it; for I . . . trust in God. And when I observe that there is great frugality, as well as wisdom in His works, since He has been evidently sparing both of labor and materials; for by the various wonderful inventions of propagation He has provided for the continual peopling His world with plants and animals, without being at the trouble of repeated new creations; and by the natural reduction of, compound substances to their original elements, capable of being employed in new compositions, He has prevented the necessity of creating new matter; so that the earth, water, air and perhaps fire, which being compounded from wood, do, when the wood is dissolved return and again become air, earth, fire and water; I say that when I see nothing annihilated, and not even a drop of water wasted, I cannot suspect the annihilation of souls, or believe that He will suffer the daily waste of millions of minds ready made that now exist and put Himself to the continual trouble of making new ones. Thus finding myself to exist in the world, I believe I shall in some shape or other, always exist; and, with all the inconveniences human life is liable to, I shall not object to a new edition of mine; hoping, however, that the errata of the last may be corrected.

BENJAMIN FRANKLIN

I came from God
and I'm going back to God,
and I won't have any gaps of death
in the middle of my life.

GEORGE MACDONALD

We cannot describe the natural history of the soul, but
we know that it is divine. I cannot tell if these wonderful
qualities which house today in this mortal frame shall ever
re-assemble in equal activity in a similar frame, or whether
they have before had a natural history like that of this body
you see before you; but this one thing I know, that these
qualities did not now begin to exist, cannot be sick with my
sickness, nor buried in any grave; but that they circulate
through the universe; before the world was they were.
Nothing can bar them out, or shut them in, but they
penetrate the ocean and land, space and time, form an
essence and hold the key to universal nature. I draw from
this faith, courage, and hope. All things are known to the
soul. It is not to be surprised by any communication.
Nothing can be greater than it. Let those fear and those
fawn who will. The soul is in her native realm, and it is
wider than space, older than time, wide as hope, rich as
love. Pusillanimity and fear she refuses with a beautiful
scorn; they are not for her who puts on her coronation robes
and goes out through universal love to universal power.

RALPH WALDO EMERSON

HOW BEAUTIFUL TO BE WITH GOD

How beautiful to be with God,
    When earth is fading like a dream,
And from this mist-encircled shore
    We launch upon the unknown stream.

No doubt, no fear, no anxious care,
    But comforted by staff and rod,
In the faith-brightened hour of death
    How beautiful to be with God.

Then let it fade, this dream of earth,
    When I have done my lifework here,
Or long, or short, as seemeth best—
    What matters so God's will appear.

I will not fear to launch my bark,
    Upon the darkly rolling flood,
'Tis but to pierce the mist—and then
    How beautiful to be with God.

W. HALSEY SMITH

ACKNOWLEDGMENTS

The editor and the publisher have made every effort to trace the ownership of all copyrighted material and to secure permission from copyright holders of such material. In the event of any question arising as to the use of any material the publisher and editor, while expressing regret for inadvertent error, will be pleased to make the necessary corrections in future printings. Thanks are due to the following authors, publications and agents for permission to use the material indicated.

AMERICAN ETHICAL UNION, for excerpt from *Life and Destiny* by Felix Adler, copyright © 1944 by American Ethical Union. All rights reserved.

BEACON PRESS, for excerpt from *Man's Search for Meaning* by Viktor Frankl, copyright © 1959, 1962 by Viktor Frankl.

THE DEVIN-ADAIR CO., INC., for excerpt by Austin O'Malley from *Keystones of Thought*, copyright by The Devin-Adair Co., Inc.

E. P. DUTTON, for excerpt from *An Airman's Letter to His Mother*, copyright © 1940 by E. P. Dutton.

FOUNDATION FOR CHRISTIAN LIVING, for excerpt from *Eternal Life* by Dr. Norman Vincent Peale, copyright © 1977 by Norman Vincent Peale.

HARPER & ROW, PUBLISHERS, INC., for excerpt from *The Bridge of San Luis Rey* by Thornton Wilder, copyright © 1927 by Albert and Charles Boni, Inc. Renewed 1955 by Thornton Wilder; for "To Those Left Behind" from *Facing the Stars* by Grace Noll Crowell, copyright © 1941 by Harper & Row, Publishers, Inc.; for excerpt from *You Can't Go Home Again* by Thomas Wolfe, copyright © 1934, 1937, 1938, 1940 by Maxwell Perkins as Executor, renewed 1968 by Paul Gitlin; for excerpt from *Place of Worship in Modern Medicine* by Howard Collier as quoted in *The Choice Is Always Ours*, edited by Dorothy Berkley Phillips, copyright © 1948 by Dorothy B. Phillips.

HARTMORE HOUSE, for excerpts by Gene E. Bartlett and Wernher von Braun from *A Treasury of the Art of Living*, edited by Sidney Greenberg, copyright © 1963 by Hartmore House.

HILL AND WANG (a division of Farrar, Straus & Giroux, Inc.), for a selection from "Uncle Vanya" from *Anton Chekov: Four Plays*, translated by David Magarshack, copyright © 1960, 1969 by David Magarshack.

THE HOGARTH PRESS LTD., for excerpt from Edwin Muir's *Autobiography*.

HOLT, RINEHART AND WINSTON, for "Acceptance" by Robert Frost from *The Poetry of Robert Frost*, edited by Edward Connery Lathem, copyright © 1928, 1969 by Holt, Rinehart and Winston, © 1956 by Robert Frost.

JAMES KIRKUP, for "There Is a New Morning," "The Vision of Paradise" and "He Who Asked."

ALFRED A. KNOPF, INC., for "With Love" by Leonora Speyer from *Slow Wall. Together With Nor Without Music and Further Poems*, by Leonora Speyer, copyright © 1939, 1946, 1951 by Leonora Speyer, and renewed 1967, 1974, by the Estate of Leonora Speyer.

LONGMAN GROUP, LIMITED, for excerpt from *The Book On the Craft of Dying* by F.M.M. Comper; for selection by Dean Inge from *Survival and Immortality*.

NATIONAL SELECTED MORTICIANS, for "How Beautiful to Be with God" by W. Halsey Smith, from *A Service Book*, copyright © 1953.

NEW DIRECTIONS PUBLISHING CORPORATION, for "The Heavenly City" by Stevie Smith from *Selected Poems*, copyright © 1962 by Stevie Smith.

PANTHEON BOOKS (a division of Random House, Inc.), for "Testament" ("These Too, I Leave to You") by Anne Morrow Lindbergh, copyright © 1941 by Anne Morrow Lindbergh. Reprinted from *The Unicorn and Other Poems* by Anne Morrow Lindbergh.

CHARLES SCRIBNER'S SONS, for "O World" ("The Soul's Invincible Surmise") by George Santayana from *Poems*, copyright © 1923 by Charles Scribner's Sons.

THE VIKING PRESS, INC., for "Weep Not, Weep Not . . . Go Down Death" from *God's Trombones* by James Weldon Johnson, copyright © 1927 by The Viking Press, Inc., © 1955 by Grace Nail Johnson.

Designed by Thomas James Aaron
Illustrated by Lynn Sweat
Type set in Zapf International Light
A face designed by Herman Zapf
Printed by Federated Lithographers –Printers, Inc.